sweet and sour

sweet and sour

MAHDIA DAQIQ

SWEET AND SOUR

iUniverse books may be ordered through booksellers or by contacting:

iUniverse
1663 Liberty Drive
Bloomington, IN 47403
www.iuniverse.com
1-800-Authors (1-800-288-4677)

ISBN: 978-1-5320-2979-0 (sc)
ISBN: 978-1-5320-2980-6 (e)

Print information available on the last page.

iUniverse rev. date: 08/14/2017

A cup of tea

Full inside
Red as the moon in the late afternoons
Hot as the sun on a summer day
It kisses my lips
and goes down through my throat
Like fire
Sweet and sour
Dark as the night
Full of sweet sprinkle of stars
A cup full of dark black tea
Warms the heart of a beast
A cup of tea

She is not a prostitute

She came to you to work
But you closed the door
You told her to be a whore
That night,
When she was back
You told her
Your stuff is packed, she begged
But you shook your head
In the middle of the night
She didn't know where to hide
From the boys on the side
The cars stopped by her
"Do you need a ride?"
She stopped and cried
But they made fun of her
"Are you gonna be with me tonight?"
She is not a prostitute
She came to ask for help
Ashhh, be quiet
Nobody heard her voice
The end of a strong fight

I believe in myself

When I was a child
I wished I was never born
Sometimes
I wished to be a boy
I wished to be invisible
I wished to be anything except a woman
I hated my body
This was what they thought of me
I hated to listen to the news
Every day there was something
To make me hate myself more
But no more
I believe in myself
And this is important for me
I believe in myself
And I will make the world believe in me
I believe in myself

Fall

I learned from the fall
To be ready for changes
I learned from the trees
To grow again after each winter
I learned from the last leaves
To not be afraid of any storm and winds
I learned from myself
Life is short and too precious to be wasted
I learned from the change
To take a lesson from every loss
I learned from the fall
Things are always going to change

Rokhshana

Sitting on the ground
She shut her eyes.
They dug her a grave
She thought
Maybe someone will stop them
Someone who is not just humane but knows
humanity
He pulled her arm and walked her to the grave
They put her on the grave
She looked at each and every one of them
Smiled, and knew there was no human in that mob
But only beasts who were full of guilt
Her dad's head was down
Crystal clear water coming out of his eyes
But his mouth was shut
Her mom was screaming in pain
She promised she would not cry
Not even ask for help
She just looked at their eyes
As the stones ran over her
Her bleeding head couldn't hold it any longer
She kept her head up
The last stone came
Her holy body fell down and never stood up.

A girl

When a girl is born
A mother will smile
Because she knows now she has someone who can
feel her
When a girl is born
A father will smile
Because he knows now he has someone to help him
When a girl is born
A brother will smile
Because he finds a kind partner to play with
When a girl is born
A sister will smile
Because she knows she will have a best friend
When a girl is born
Thousands of lives will be born with her
A woman is a life

We are one

Stop closing your windows and shutting your door
Stop drawing lines
Stop making boxes
Stop stopping yourself
Stop borders
Teach me how to say "hi"
Don't tell me to stay away from strangers
People are good
Call your friends
Clean the lines
Destroy the walls
Stand up for me
Stand up for yourself
We are one
We are good
We have love
It is enough for all of us
Show them to the world
We are one.

A poem

A poem is a feeling
A feeling in a song
The beats of a heart
A poet is a god
A poet feels the pain
The poem is a solution
Or plenty of questions
A poem is right
A poem is a heart

What I need from this life

What I need from this life
Is a nice warm room in the winter
A beautiful tree in spring
A singing bird in summer
A beautiful twilight in fall
What I need from this life is
Hands of my mother always on my shoulders
My childhood friends in the streets
A clean notebook
To lock these memories
And to unlock them when I grow up
To smile for a moment
These are
What I need from this world

The last thought

If this was my last day
My last dream
My last chance
My last breath
I would save this moment to think about you

The world is beautiful

The stars are shining
The earth is holding me
The birds are singing
The sun is shining
The trees are growing
There can be a reason to be sad
Or mad
But there is always a reason to smile
Don't miss the happiness to be sad
Even at nights when I can't see anything
I can see the whole universe above my head
Every piece of this world is a surprise
Every piece of this world is beautiful
The world is beautiful

It is snowing

Under the sky
Under the cold hearts
It is snowing
The paths are freezing cold
The prostitute is not sleeping in the streets
The doctor is out of town
And a beggar lies by the door
It is snowing
The neighbor's children are drinking hot chocolate
I can see the breaths of the merchant
And her daughter
She always wears red boots
White silk sweater
Her teeth shine brighter than snow
It is snowing
On the other side
The match sales girl is standing on the corner
With no boots
Wearing a ripped dress
It is snowing
I close the windows

Somewhere in this world

I am somewhere
In this universe
In one of those Galaxies
There is a small planet
Called Earth
I am somewhere
Under the sky
In front of the sun
I am somewhere
Sitting
While everything is moving
The sun
Moon
Earth
Time
The most important one is my life
I am somewhere
In here
Maybe
Sitting behind a tree
Thinking of the world
I am somewhere
In here
I am somewhere
In this world

Winter

Outside my window
Branch of wild trees
Each branch looks like a razor
In the cold weather
Outside my window
Dark gray sky
And the sun
That you can never see
Outside my window
People aren't walking
Nobody lives in that house
At seven o'clock there is a man
Who cleans the road
He uses any opportunity
To put his hands in his pockets
Outside my window
It is winter

The bright Kabul

Look at the stars
On the bright nights
Find out the love
In Kabul heights
35 years of fights
But, still bright
New chapters arrive
Love in lives
A sky full of kites
Babies with smiles
These are our rights

Stand up to live

Life is hard
Too difficult for a child
Too complicated for an adult
Like today's problems
It looks small
But it can make up your life
This day makes your life
And these small problems make your days
Maybe, today,
Someone told you something that hurts you
Or someone is too rude
Or someone makes you feel bad
Or you are alone
These look small
But they can slow down a mountain from rising
A tree from growing
A lion from ruling
The sun from shining
A war from winning
So be brave
Fight back
If something is bothering you,
Stop it
If someone is cruel
Stand up
If you are being used
Say no
Don't tolerate anything
Trust yourself
You are only responsible for yourself
So rule you the way you want

My Mind

My mind is my power
You can't take it from me
It is my right to think
It is part of my body
You can't tell me to stop thinking
Even if you force me to do what you want
Even if you force me to accept what you say
Even if I was your servant and you hit me every day
You can not change my thoughts
Never
I will think
I will dream big
I will get out of this
And I will change the world
With my mind
Even if my body is in prison
My mind is free
And it flies higher and higher every day
Until a time will come
When you can not fight it anymore
You have to accept it
You can't ignore it
And I am going to rule you
With my mind

Today

When you sit on that bed
Think what you did today
Maybe you will die tomorrow
Live for today
Never make your tomorrow today
It is always in our minds
That yesterday was bad
That tomorrow is good
Today will be your yesterday
And tomorrow will be your today
Again and again and again
find your today
Your whole life is today
Your tomorrow is today
Your yesterday is today
Do what you want
Tomorrow there will be no chance for you
Get up and live for today

Dream your dream

Live like your life is a dream
You will get up tomorrow
Then dream the way you want
Control your dream
Be happy
The problems are just nightmares
But you are dreaming
Fight with them they way you want to
Be yourself
Because it is just a dream
It will never repeat again
Make it a sweet dream
Because life is a dream
Life is your dream

Be yourself

While it is hard
Don't change a piece of it
Don't question it
Don't regret it
Simply love it
Be yourself
Even if you think someone is better than you
Even if everybody prefers others over you
don't change it
A math teacher can't be a language teacher
If they try they will be a worse teacher
But they can be best at math
You have something inside you
That is made just for you
You can be best at it
But if you try to change it
You will lose it
You will lose yourself
Every day you will have a new personality
Never do it
Let people know you
Let the person inside you

Be a human

Being a human
Doesn't mean having a human body
It means to have the heart of a human
To be the one who helps
The one who never puts someone else lower than themselves
The one who speaks up for others
The one who feels
The one who can cry for others
The one who doesn't know race, gender, color
The one who wants peace and stands for it
The one who doesn't believe in borders
The one who is a human

Smile

One smile can change your life
Smile to your enemies it shows how big you are
Smile to your friends, it shows how close you are
Smile to the problems, it shows how strong you are
Smile to your achievements, it shows how hard you work
Smile when you win, it shows how happy you are
Smile when you lose, it shows how strong you are
Smile to change the world and change your life.

My fears

I am not afraid of religion
I am afraid of people's interpretation of religion
I am not afraid of fights
I am afraid of the reasons to fight
I am not afraid of voice
I am afraid of the tone of the voice
I am not afraid of thoughts
I am afraid of the root of the thoughts
I am not afraid of beliefs
I am afraid of believing the unknown
I am not afraid of humans
I am afraid of a human with no humanity

A (Wo)man

I am a woman
Am I just for serving you?
A servant or a slave whose job is obeying you?
I am a human, but
Am I not as respectable as you?
A joke, that has lots of truth
Human just by name, and human which is you.
Like a king and his servants
A king who inherits his throne
Having the life he wants to
Demanding people what to do
His dreams always become true
A slave who is forced to give
His life, his energy, his meaning to you
This is the story of me and you
You being a man and I being a woman
You can do the things you want to
Of course, the society has boundaries, even for you
But when it is me
The boundaries get tighter
The society gets more aware
My acts get questioned
My behaviors get judged
The road that is flat for you
Becomes a steep hill for me
My dreams get harder to reach
Long story short, you can continue.
But of course, I won't let you anymore.

Life

Life
Is
A paper
No pen
No pencil
Just you
Enough for a life to be written

Myself and her

I love her
She always refuses to be me
I love her when she smiles
Sometimes she gets angry
Sometimes she gets lost
When I lose her
I try everyone else to replace her
New personalities
New hobbies
But I continue feeling lost
Like a fish in an empty ocean
Like a book without any words
Like a country girl in a big city
Without her, I am meaningless
But she comes back
Because she knows, I will need her
She is my true self
The one that I am afraid of
Maybe she is not good enough
Strong enough
Smart enough
I always tried to change her
Ignored her talents
Brought her down
But I always ended up back to her
Because she is my true self

I will reach

Step by step
Word to word
Breath to breath
I will go
I will run
I will fly
I will fail
I will continue
From each way
From all ways
I will break the mountains
I will swim the ocean
I will pass the storms
I will go
Until I reach

Free

I think
I am free
I let myself be free
Free from you
Free from me
I let it go

I write about you

I want to write for a woman
I grab a pen, pencil, and paper
I know every word
One by one
Word by word
It is painful
I write with the pen
The pen can't handle it
It cries all of its colors out
I write with a pencil
The pencil crashes under the pain
I write with a feather dipped in ink
The feather is too delicate
The ink is too bloody
It bleeds
I try to say it
You are too strong for words
There is no word for you
Only the heart and mind
Can handle you
The minds that are open for you
And the hearts that can feel you

Take care

You will lose
You will die
So, don't care
Just live high
Live for yourself
Sometimes
Ask yourself
How are you?
Are you happy?
Are you sad?
Are you feeling something bad?
Because you need yourself
To live
Take care of it
Don't make yourself unhappy
Because that is the only thing you are living for

Dark side

Turn to the dark side
There are little crystal stars
Shiny yellow moon
Making something big like the sun
It will come to an end soon
The sun is always one
It is hard to keep it up in the afternoon
Turn on to the dark side
There are stars that you keep far
Bring them close, where you are
The sun is the smallest between the stars
But you hide them under a blinding sun
There is not one
Turn to dark side
And find the brightness

I am sorry, mom.

I am sorry, mom.
because you've done a lot for me
But I can't do anything for you
I am sorry, mom
Because you spent your whole life for me
And I never had time for you
I am sorry, mom
I know you rejected your dreams instead you helped
me reach mine
I feel you, when you are hungry
But you eat nothing because you want your child to
eat
And you tell us, smiling, "I am not hungry"
I feel you, when you see a beautiful dress
But you don't buy it instead you always bought
something better for us
I feel you when you are cold, but you don't tell
anybody, instead
You want your child to be warm and wear your
jacket
Thank you, mom.

Printed in the United States
By Bookmasters

Printed in the United States
By Bookmasters